ZIMBABWEAN ODYSSEY

The sequel

By

Sheila V. Hartwell

Shield Crest

© Copyright 2018 Sheila Hartwell

All rights reserved

ISBN: 978-1-912505-41-8

MMXVIII

A CIP catalogue record for this book
is available from the British Library

Published by
ShieldCrest Publishing Ltd.,
Aylesbury, Buckinghamshire,
HP18 0TF England
Tel: +44 (0) 333 8000 890
www.shieldcrest.co.uk

Dedicated to
the 'Lost Tribe of Africa'
whoever you are, wherever you are -
yearning always for those
'great spaces washed with sun'*

(*The Burial, Rudyard Kipling 1922)

ABOUT THE AUTHOR

Sheila was born in the fifties in Rhodesia, now Zimbabwe. At eight years old she and her siblings were placed in care. After nine years at the Rhodesia Children's Home she left to attend college where she gained a diploma in secretarial skills which saw her in good stead throughout her working career.

Sheila's great passions are art, photography, elephants and Zimbabwe, her beloved homeland.

After six years under the Mugabe regime she and her husband, Mike, left Zimbabwe to settle in the UK where they remain today.

CONTENTS

PROLOGUE

PART 1

    I. Returning to the Fold
   II. Moving On
  III. Working Girl
  IV. The Bush War (Second Chimurenga)
   V. European Adventure
  VI. The Whitsun Foundation
 VII. The Deafening Silence
VIII. End of the Bush War
  IX. Mike
   X. Cerebral Malaria
  XI. Easther
 XII. UK Bound

PART 2

Reunion

PROLOGUE

"I felt like I was in Zimbabwe with the writer ... and felt I could reach out and touch this country ..."

"it's an uplifting and inspirational message for the human soul and life in general in the most difficult to times ... those wonderful descriptions of the animals, landscape, fragrances, people, fun and fear in a roller-coaster of emotion made me truly believe I strode every step in time around this amazing yet troubled country she calls home ... it made me smile, it made me giggle and it made me cry ..."

"The only fault with this book is that it ended – I want more!"

Although my first book *My Zimbabwean Odyssey* had, in the main, received good reviews there were some criticisms, mainly from those closest to me, with some saying I didn't portray myself as the person they know today. But that's just it, I am not the same person I was all those years ago and my book revolved around that particular period in my life right up until the time I left the Rhodesia Children's Home in 1969 at the age of 17.

Hopefully, this sequel will satisfy those readers who felt they had been left 'in mid-air' at the end of MZO and were keen to know what happened to me after leaving the Home. You will meet characters who influenced my life greatly and I hope too, as with my first book, my love for Zimbabwe will continue to shine through, not only in the words but also through my watercolours which, hopefully, will portray the vibrant tapestry that is Zimbabwe.

As a third generation Zimbabwean I have always regarded the country as my spiritual home. My birth and, indeed, virtually every white in Rhodesia was as a result of British colonialism. However, once Britain had relinquished her rule over Rhodesia these white Africans, Britain's kith and kin, felt as though they were left 'high and dry' by Britain who even made it extremely difficult, if not impossible, for some of those whites wishing to settle in the UK post-independence. Now, scattered throughout the world, these '*white skins with African souls*' have had to make new lives for themselves.

Sadly, it seems in Africa the colour of one's skin determines whether you belong or not. Interestingly, the three main cultures of Matabele, Mashona and Whites were actually all immigrants to the region between the Limpopo and Zambezi. Perhaps it's just as well then, for the Mashona and Matabeles at least, 'tribe' doesn't come into it for the true original inhabitants of the land between the Limpopo and Zambezi were the Bushmen who reigned supreme 2000 years ago. Evidence of this timid people can still be found throughout Zimbabwe today by way of caves adorned with rock paintings, the colours of which were taken from distillations of lichens, herbs, bark and berries. One such place, Domboshava, 'Dombo' meaning 'rock' and 'Shava (pronounced

'Shawa') meaning 'red', lying about 20 miles north of Harare, consists of caves with paintings dating back almost 6,000 years.

Domboshava

For those unfamiliar with the early history of Rhodesia I share with you an extract from the Africa Institute Bulletin[1]

'Modern Rhodesian history dates back to the Matabele migration from the Transvaal in the late 1830s when they arrived in the area now known as Bulawayo. The Matabele, a scion of the Zulu nation, under their Chief Mzilikaze, were driven from

---

[1] Africa Institute Bulletin, Vol 15, 1977 - Rhodesia - Mzilikaze to Smith

the Transvaal after attacks on the Voortrekkers. Their encroachment on the land north of the Limpopo marks that first repercussion white settlement in Southern Africa was to have on the course of Rhodesian history.

The Matabele were a predatory race and established themselves in their new environment by subjugating the original inhabitants until they were firmly entrenched as rulers of the territory between the Limpopo and Zambezi rivers. Their impis foraged far and wide across the land, looting cattle and capturing women and children. Before the coming of the Matabele the Bushmen, who left their paintings in remote caves, and the negro-hamitic peoples who had migrated from the lakes of Central Africa were the occupants of Rhodesia. This migration
brought the Mashona to Rhodesia, possibly sometime in the 1500s. There were also the builders of Great Zimbabwe and numerous other imposing stone structures who left no other record of their passing, save the silent ruins scattered about the land. By the last half of the 19th century when whites started taking an interest in the land north of the Limpopo the Matabele and the Mashona were already firmly established in the area.

The first whites to reach Rhodesia were missionaries, hunters and trekkers who crossed the Limpopo in search of grazing. The first actual white settlers in 1890 took part in what is termed the scramble for Africa, preceded and triggered off by the discovery of diamonds and gold in South Africa. During the 1880s European imperial powers like Germany, Portugal and Britain showed a growing interest in land north of the Limpopo.

The Portuguese already had colonies on the East and West coasts of Southern and Central Africa and British penetration from the south was to prevent them from linking their territories across Africa. Germany found herself in much the same position as Portugal and her interest in the Transvaal Republic was growing steadily. Transvaal too had put out tentative feelers towards the north, which could ultimately have led to the linking of German and Transvaal territory, thereby severing the path of British advancement.

Such was the position in the 1880s when Cecil John Rhodes, politician and mining magnate, who gave his name to Rhodesia, decided to act. John Smith Moffat, at the instigation of Rhodes persuaded Lobengula, who had succeeded Mzilikaze in 1868, to sign the Moffat Treaty in 1888. In terms of the treaty the Matabele agreed not to enter into correspondence or treaty with any foreign power without the sanction of the British High Commissioner for South Africa.

The Transvaal and Portuguese Governments both objected to the Moffat Treaty, but the British Government remained adamant.

Later during the same year British advancement into Central Africa was finally secured when Lobengula signed the Rudd Concession giving Rhodes 'complete and exclusive charge over all metal and mineral rights' in Rhodesia in return for a monthly payment of £100 to himself and his heirs. In addition to this, Lobengula received 1,000 rifles and 100,000 rounds of ammunition.

Besides mineral rights, the Rudd Concession also conferred sweeping commercial and legal powers on Rhodes. Armed with the Concession, Rhodes used his considerable financial resources, derived from control of De Beers and Gold Fields of South Africa, to form the British South Africa Company (BSAC) that subsequently obtained a charter from Queen Victoria in 1899. The charter granted the BSAC the right to operate in all Southern Africa, north of Bechuanaland (Botswana), north and west of the Zuid-Afrikaanse Republiek (Transvaal) and west of the Portuguese possessions. No northern limit was stipulated.

The first pioneer column, 180 men and 500 troops in employ of the BSAC left Kimberley for Rhodesia in May 1890 and established Fort Victoria in August 1890. A party of pioneers, including the famous hunter, Courtney Selous, continued further northwards and in September 1890 raised the British flag at what is now Salisbury'.

Part 1

I

Returning to the Fold

I had returned to the family fold in 1967, two years before leaving the Rhodesia Children's Home when I began holidaying with my aunt Val, my father's younger sister, and her family. Whether it was because I was being prepared for a life outside the confines of the Home or whether it was, perhaps, guilt on Val's part, I don't know, as I had always suspected she was the one who alerted the Social Welfare to our plight all those years ago. My suspicion followed a recollection she shared with me when in the late 1950's she popped in unannounced to our house in Braeside only to find my parents out drinking whilst we children were left starving as food burned on the stove. She never forgave them for it and, indeed, I never held the tip-off to the Social Welfare against her as I would probably have done the same in her shoes.

During those holidays I was happy to be reunited with my grandmother who lived in a big old Rhodesian house on the corner of Montagu Avenue and Salisbury Street in what was, and still is, known as 'The Avenues' where houses nestle amongst tree-lined avenues of jacarandas and flamboyants.

Jacarandas in bloom

When in bloom the trees transformed the rather dreary roads into rich tapestries of purples and vibrant reds, the fallen blossom beneath mirroring their colours.

The Jacaranda is native to South America, Brazil in particular, and was first planted in Rhodesia in the late 1800s. Exotic trees such as the Jacaranda and Flamboyant ('flame tree'), native to Madagascar, are casualties in the current drive to rid the country of 'alien' species of trees, replacing them with indigenous varieties - mopane, msasa, marula and lucky bean tree, to name a few. Many of these indigenous trees have their own exquisite beauty and uses. The msasa, a firm favourite of mine, densely covers the woodlands of Zimbabwe.

From mid-September and through October its array of colours - reds, yellows, burnt oranges and claret - transform the landscape into a masterpiece. It is host to the hairy orangey-yellow Msasa worm which makes up part of the diet of the rural population. I'm told, too, that chewing the stripped bark of the msasa is very good in relieving constipation ...... now they tell me!!

Flamboyants in bloom

The Mopane tree, prolific in the Zambezi Valley and a major source of food for elephants, hosts the Mopane Worm (Madora), larvae of the Mopane Emperor Moth. A large edible caterpillar it is also a staple for the locals, providing much needed protein and nutrients. The Lucky Bean Tree, also known as Munhimbiti in Shona and Umgqogqogqo in Ndebele, is normally found in

3

open woodland or rocky terrains. It has scarlet red flowers with orangey-red and black seeds which can be made into necklaces which are worn in many African cultures to ward off evil spirits. I was thrilled to find one of these trees in Harare on my recent visit, and took the opportunity of photographing its radiant scarlet flowers against the azure blue sky.

A typical 'old Rhodesian' building my grandmother's house had a highly polished red flagstone verandah virtually all the way around it. It also came with its own provenance, being the house Cecil John Rhodes stayed in on his treks from South Africa up to Rhodesia, a country he was keen to develop, particularly the railway, to fulfil his 'Cape to Cairo Railway' dream. Even the enormous old tree used to tether the oxen still stood in the garden.

Of course, with provenance came publicity and the house generated a lot of interest with the media, both Press and television. How my '*no nonsense, what you see is what you get*' grandmother coped with all the attention I shudder to think! Every room was filmed, including the bedrooms where each room had its own fireplace surrounded by intricately painted tiles.

With all but one of her children having left home my grandmother and her youngest son, Andy, rattled around its large rooms. Andy was her 'laat lammetjie', Afrikaans for 'late baby'. Being younger than most of his nieces and nephews we all thought of him as more of a cousin than uncle! An avid music collector with a vinyl record collection many would die for I remember, whilst visiting on one of my holidays from the Home, Andy asking me to paint a mural of Jimi Hendrix on his bedroom wall, which I did - what Rhodes would have thought of the psychedelic image I hate to think! Another of his passions was his 'dagga' (cannibas) plants which he interspersed amongst my grandmother's shrubs and flowers. On one occasion he gingerly shadowed my grandmother, whose eyesight was failing badly, as she walked my great aunt Winnie around the garden. As she stopped beside the thriving dagga plants she exclaimed *"Aren't my dahlias coming up lovely Winnie?"*.

Example of a typical old Rhodesian house similar to my grandmother's

Sadly, after my grandmother died the historic house was demolished and in its place today stands a petrol station.

II

Moving on

I t was the end of 1969 and I thought "Well, this is it" as one door closed and another opened. Picking up my suitcase and making my way down the stairs out of Davies House I was finally leaving the familiarity of the Rhodesia Children's Home and beginning a new life in the outside world.

A place had already been booked for me at the Lady Stanley Girl's Club, my first year's accommodation being paid for by the Home whilst I attended the Polytechnic to do a one-year secretarial course. Lady Stanley was a stepping stone for most of the girls leaving the Home and going onto college or starting jobs. By the time I was admitted there weren't any other girls from the Home as they had either got married or, once having left college and earning, moved into places of their own. Now I would be amongst girls mainly from farming backgrounds who, after leaving boarding school, also needed somewhere in the city to lodge whilst at college or work.

Upon arrival at the hostel I was introduced to the live-in supervisor, Mrs Cave, a tall, thin and rather austere looking woman, who showed me to my room which I was told I would be sharing with a girl called Ainsley-Jane. My first night at the hostel mirrored that of my first night at the Home all those years ago. I hardly slept. As daylight broke and rays of sunshine filtered through the window on that first Sunday morning I hurriedly got dressed awaiting the bell for breakfast which meant the front door being unlocked thus enabling me to slip out to my Aunt Val's house a short distance away. The sunshine-filled room, however, gave the impression it was a lot later than it actually was and not having a watch little did I realise I would have to wait another four hours or so before scuttling down the road! With time to kill I began to reflect on my new roommate. What was she like? Was she much older than me and, more importantly, would we get on? But I needn't have worried. When Ainsley-Jane returned that evening she made me feel quite at ease. After introductions we spent the next couple of hours learning more about each other. She told me everyone called her AJ and I learned she was a hairdresser and had recently got engaged. With her fiancé based in Sinoia she spent every weekend there. We became firm friends and it was only when she left to get married I decided to move into one of the single rooms at the hostel.

With the strict confines of the Home behind me it took a fair amount of time getting used to being a free spirit and making my own decisions. I still had to meet with the Social Welfare once a month, something I didn't relish, resenting the fact that the young girl I was accountable to had barely sipped life herself so what she really knew about it was anyone's guess.

As time went on I began to realise that beneath her aloof exterior Mrs Cave was a truly likeable, genuine and approachable person, becoming a real friend and confidant to most of us girls. Her office, which doubled-up as reception, was always welcoming and it wasn't unusual for any of us to pop in and occupy the spare seat beside her desk, passing the time of day with chitter-chatter. It was here at reception where all visitors and telephone calls were announced over the public address system. Excited, girls would dash downstairs to meet boyfriends or take phone calls on the public telephone in one corner of the foyer. With the majority of young men in the Forces it wasn't uncommon for groups of them, whilst on 'R&R' (rest and recreation) from the war, to phone up for blind dates whereupon a handful of us girls would hurriedly get ready for a night out on the town. One of our favourite outings was the Airforce Base at New Serum near Salisbury Airport. The name 'New Sarum' was derived from Salisbury's sister city in Wiltshire, England, where the RAF Station near Wiltshire was called 'Old Sarum' and, due to the close association between the two air force bases, it was decided the new airfield in Salisbury be called 'New Sarum'. We always looked forward to these outings, especially the 'hooligan juice', a mixture of champagne and ice-cream, which we'd down like milkshakes and end up feeling the worse for wear afterwards!

Occasionally, the odd (pun intended!) individual would phone up for a date. Irritated by one persistent caller we decided to pull a prank which involved Mrs Cave's dog Mandy, a golden Labrador. We told him a girl was interested in going out with him and gave Mandy's name, describing her as blonde, easy-going and easily recognisable as she would probably be lying on the carpet when he arrived!! Needless to say, the poor chap was none too pleased when he arrived but it did put a stop to his calls!

Off reception was the dining room and lounge area. The dining room always buzzed with excitement and chitter-chatter, particularly in the evenings when the sharing of one's day or the anticipation of a date had everyone in high spirits. Mrs Cave had her own table which was situated next to the French door leading to the back garden of the hostel. She had a penchant for vitamins and each mealtime would have various tubs of vitamins lined up like little soldiers which she dutifully took. With such a slim frame we were surprised she didn't rattle! Whenever at the table she would have her dog, Thor, a Belgian Shepherd who replaced Mandy, lying at her feet. Whilst having lunch one day I recall Mrs Cave suddenly shooting up, opening the door and shoving Thor out. She beckoned to one of us to assist her in pulling on a piece of string which dangled from his rear end. You can imagine our response! Not only were we mortified but also paralytic with nervous laughter as we went round the table to find a taker. "*You do it*", "*No, you do it*" we all shouted at one another by which time Mrs Cave was running low on patience. With no takers she volunteered Claire, a shy and unassuming girl, to assist. Going nowhere near his rear end poor Claire, amidst raucous laughter filtering out of the dining room and with a face as red as a beetroot, held tightly onto the dog whilst Mrs Cave tugged on the seemingly endless piece of string! Needless to say, it put most of us off our food and I, for one, never looked at Mrs Cave or, indeed spaghetti, in the same way again!

The hostel had about a dozen maids, all of whom shared a dormitory downstairs off the back of the kitchen/utility area. Some were cleaners whilst others worked in the kitchen and served at the tables. If the maids wished, they could take on our laundry to bring in extra money. Being at college and having very little money in my first year I wasn't able to afford the luxury of a maid, however, shortly after starting my first job I was approached by Phyllis the oldest of all the maids. She was a timid little soul with a weathered and wrinkly face. She would collect my washing a couple of times a week in the mornings and return it later in the day in neat, crisply ironed piles. I was surprised at how adept she was in tackling any task, not only considering her age but also the fact that she had only one hand, her right one missing at the wrist. I never drew attention to her affliction and to this day am none the wiser as to what befell her.

Once I started working I was able to save up and buy my first car, a mini. Being an early version it had a long gear stick coming up from the floor and horizontal sliding windows. It wasn't in the best of condition, however, the sense of freedom and independence it gave was great, not to mention the sudden increase in friends at the hostel! I loved driving them around, our favourite outings being the drive-in restaurants which were plentiful at the time, the Blue Gardinia, Yellow Orchard and, our absolute favourite, The Gremlin, to name a few. It was at The Gremlin where the 'FLICK your lights for service' sign would take on a very different meaning if one wasn't parked head-on with it! Drive-In Cinemas were popular too. Originally an American idea, the drive-in was a cheap way to see a movie with the charge being per car rather than per person. So it wasn't unusual seeing cars with bodies packed in like sardines, the idea being once they were parked they could escape the car, plonk themselves down in an empty space next to a speaker and picnic under the stars whilst watching the movie. The drive-in consisted of rows upon rows of humps - a bit like 'sleeping policemen', but a lot bigger - which we would drive up and stop when full-on with the huge screen ahead. As if this wasn't bad enough, we also had to negotiate getting as close as possible to the post which held the speaker. Once satisfied with the maneouvre the window would be wound down slightly and the speaker safely attached. Many a time folk would forget the speaker when driving off, ripping it from its post! Needless to say, drive-ins were a firm favourite of courting couples, their cars easily spotted by their steamed-up windows!

Life at the hostel was never dull. I remember one group of girls growing a dagga (cannibas) plant which they named Geronimo and whenever the Police were called out, for whatever reason, all you could hear ringing through the hostel was *"Geronimo!, Geronimo!"*, being the signal to hide the plant as quickly as possible!

Occasionally, girls holidaying in Rhodesia would stay at the hostel. Nicky, a friend, and I decided to accompany two girls, Jane from Kent in the UK and Judy her South African cousin, on a camping trip to Lake Kariba in the Zambezi Valley. As Jane had never seen elephants in the wild before we thought it a good idea to head for Kariba with its plentiful wildlife and spectacular scenery.

With the car packed and Jane at the wheel the four of us made off just before dawn while it was still cool for the five hour drive to Lake Kariba. Passing through Sinoia we pointed out to our visitors the Sinoia Caves. The caves, a system of caverns, is a diver's paradise, a magnet for divers from all over the world. The walls within these caves plunge down about 45 metres into '*The Sleeping Pool*' with a depth of 80-120 metres. Shafts of sunlight filter down from the top into the Sleeping

Pool's vivid blue and crystal clear water '.... *where the quiet is so thick you can almost touch it and you whisper as if in an alien church...*'. The first white man to discover the caves was Courtney Selous in the late 19th century, although long before that they had been used by the Mashona Chief, Chinhoyi, after whom the town Sinoia was subsequently re-named, and his followers as a refuge from invading tribes.

Sleeping Pool

It was here in Sinoia the second Chimurenga (liberation war) was launched in 1966. Rumour has it my great aunt Mary, my grandmother's sister, was hanging out the washing when she heard the first gunshot. How true that is, I don't know, but, its a pretty good story!

By the time we got to Makuti, 77Kms from Lake Kariba, the wall of heat hit us. Years later on a visit to Zimbabwe from the UK I couldn't resist taking a photo

of the signpost at Makuti, particularly where the Clouds End Hotel is mentioned, a welcoming sight for any bushwacked traveller!

Sign at Makuti Turn-Off

On approaching the Lake we noticed big mounds of fresh elephant dung on the road ahead. Beside herself with excitement Jane scanned the thick vegetation on either side of the road. We told her the only way of knowing elephants were in the vicinity was to put a hand into the dung to see if it was still warm and suggested she try it. Jane was horrified, shrieking '*No way!*' As large as they are, elephants are easily camouflaged by the lush vegetation. We hadn't gone too far before Jane slammed on the breaks and shouted "*there they are!*". Barely three yards away stood a couple of elephants amongst the thicket. Mesmerised, we sat for quite a while taking in the sight before making off again, eventually arriving at the campsite at Mopani Bay on the shores of Lake Kariba - where elephants and buffaloes are known to roam around or through the camp - at about 9 o'clock just as the campers were preparing breakfast. Agreeing the tent should go up upon arrival Jane, with her 'jolly hockey sticks' manner took charge. With military precision she bellowed instructions, oblivious to the small group of men, mugs of tea in hand, gathering round to watch. We didn't disappoint on the entertainment stakes as every time we looked their way the men stood stifling their laughter which made Nicky and I self-consciously giggle our way through the painful process. By the time the tent was finally up our male audience had become acquaintances. Most of them had boats and one of them invited the four of us to spend the day tiger fishing on his, an invitation we couldn't refuse!

Despite the heat, it was wonderful being on the lake with elephants roaming on the shoreline, hippos bobbing in the shallow waters and crocodiles lazily basking on warm rocks. The stillness of mid-day exaggerated the buzzing of insects as they danced on the water's silvery surface. We caught mainly bream and the odd tiger fish, named as such due to its blue/black lateral tiger stripes, which had us girls squealing and dashing to the opposite side of the boat, leaving it listing precariously to one side. Caught mainly with kapenta (a small sardine-like fish) the tiger fish is best kept at arm's length, as being a lightning quick predatory 'game fish' with 32 razor sharp teeth it could lacerate the flesh in an instant causing damage to hands and feet. With already nine toes I didn't relish losing any more! Believe it or not, with all the other wildlife around us, it was the tiger fish we feared most!

When we returned to camp at sundown we cooked our spoils over an open fire on the shoreline. It was only when we finally returned to our tent we discovered elephants had been through the camp leaving a crumpled tent on the ground with all our smalls - bras, knickers - either scattered on the ground or hanging from guy ropes that had got tangled in the trees! We were mortified and our 'flying the flags' remained the butt of everyone's jokes for the duration!

III

Working Girl

I secured my first job at a company called SEECO whose chairman was Teddy Cohen. As a Jew and successful businessman Mr Cohen would have known a number of, if not all, the Jews who were either on the Home's committee or were Friends of the Home which accounted for the feeling of protectiveness I got from him and his PA Angie. Teddy was the first person to set-up a company providing affordable credit to the black population. Zimbabwe Furnishers had branches virtually all over the country and was synonymous with its catchy jingle '*Nyore Nyore Zimbabwe Furnishers, Nyore Nyore Zimbabwe Cha Cha Cha*'! ('nyore' meaning 'easy'). SEECO, the HQ was situated in Southampton House, a newly constructed block in the centre of Salisbury. I thought I had 'finally arrived' on my first day! For 1971, the offices were very state-of-the-art, particularly the reception area which had coloured lights down one wall, each one lighting up whenever an extension was engaged. As a junior typist I shared an office with a girl called Frankie who I was thrilled to discover went to the same high school as me. We hit it off straight away with most days being filled with light-hearted banter, much to the disapproval of Mr Hope, the Company Secretary,

17

whose office was close by. Mr Hope, also a Jew, was a humourless dour character, very strict, with a huge hooked nose which served him well as he was constantly looking down on us 'silly' girls, tutting all the while, particularly when we'd sing the Nyore Nyore jingle and shake like crazy at the 'cha cha cha' bit! With hindsight, I think it was probably the 'easy easy' bit that put the wind up him! Mr Cohen, a big bear of a man with a heart just as big, was the total opposite of 'No Hope', as we used to call him. He had an enormous office at the end of the corridor which I rarely ventured into, finding his imposing frame and huge desk pretty daunting! So you can imagine my absolute terror when he suggested to Angie that I accompany him for the day on a visit to our branch in Que Que. They obviously thought the experience would do me the world of good. Wracked with nerves and shorthand book and pencil in hand I got into his bright pink American Cadillac convertible. It truly was a beauty with its white-walled tyres and pristine shiny metalwork. I didn't have the heart or, indeed, courage to tell him I was prone to motion sickness and that throwing dictation into the mix on the couple of hour's journey to Que Que would only exacerbate things! I had never taken dictation before and the idea was that I would take notes on the journey and then type them up once in Que Que while he got on with the more important business. Anyone who has suffered car sickness will know how important it is to keep your eyes on the road. How I made it I shall never know, but it must've been the deep concentration with my shorthand that did it, not a hint of puke upon arrival! Late afternoon we made our journey back to Salisbury, stopping at a petrol station along the way. Whilst filling up Mr Cohen handed me money to get us some treats for the journey back. I felt embarrased at first, but he insisted saying I could choose anything I wanted. Needless to say, I returned with biltong, chips (crisps) Crunchy Bars and ice cold cokes. The journey back under the waning African sun was relaxed and enjoyable as we chatted endlessly, munching our way through the treats, with me thinking *'this PA malarky, even if pretend, wasn't so bad after all!!'*

But things soon took a change that would see me leaving my job. Opposite Southampton House on First Street stood the historical colonial Dominian Buildings, a double storey with a balcony overlooking First Street. In 1971 the old building was being used as one-room accommodation and I was horrified to hear, via my brothers, that my father and his new wife, Jean, were dossing down there. Apparently, my father had met Jean, a barmaid, at the well-renowned Long Bar in Meikles Hotel and, I suppose, being kindred spirits (no pun intended!) they shacked-up. Knowing they were in such close proximity left me on tenterhooks and I would daily look out the office window down on Dominian Buildings hoping and praying our paths wouldn't cross. One morning I spotted my father, cigarette in hand, hopelessly drunk and scratching his backside, wandering around the balcony in his Y-fronts. I shuddered to think what my workmates would make of it and continued to keep a low profile in the hopes he didn't track me down. Horrifyingly, my hopes were dashed when one day the Receptionist rang to say I had a couple of visitors. When approaching reception my heart sank at the sight of my father and Jean standing there. Both looked dishevelled and totally spaced out. Jean's dress was unzipped all the way down her back. I quickly hustled them out into the corridor telling them I was extremely busy and that they would have to leave. Deeply embarrased, I returned to the office fully aware their visit hadn't gone unnoticed. From then on anyone visiting me were given the 'once over' by both Angie and Mr Cohen.

It was close on eight months when I decided to move on. My decision was met with some resistance by Angie and Frankie, but Mr Cohen, encouraging my independence and resolve, agreed if that's what I wanted then so be it. I think my dubious visitors might have played a part in his encouragement! Planning my own destiny never felt so good. A friend at Lady Stanley was leaving her job to live in the UK and suggested I apply for it. I did and got the job which was at Lange Menswear in the industrial sites on the outskirts of Salisbury. Again, I was working for Jews who would undoubtedly know Teddy Cohen and, indeed, Mr Joseph, one of the Directors at Lange Menswear, was also a member of the 'Friends of the Home' group. With hindsight, it seemed that, as in my younger years, God's protection was still upon me.

IV

Bush War (Second Chimurenga)

N ick Downie states in Rhodesia Guerilla Warfare that *'One of the myths about Rhodesia is that it was a 'white man's war'. In fact 80% of the police and regular army were composed of black volunteers and of the 25,000 men on the ground at any one time, about half were Africans.'*

The Bush War, or Second Chimurenga (war of liberation), lasted about 15 years from July 1964 to December 1979. A brutal war, the atrocities of which are too graphic to mention here, was fought between the Rhodesian forces, Robert Mugabe's Zimbabwe African National Liberation Army (ZANLA), the military wing of the Zimbabwe African National Union (ZANU) and Joshua Nkomo's Zimbabwe People's Revoluntionary Army (ZIPRA), the military wing of the Zimbabwean African People's Union (ZAPU). ZANLA was supported by China and North Korea and ZIPRA by Russia. Each group fought a separate war against the Rhodesian security forces and occasionally would also fight each other!

The Rhodesian forces included the regular army, the Rhodesian Light Infantry (RLI), territorial forces and elite units such as the Rhodesian SAS, Selous Scouts and Grey Scouts. Probably the most famous and respected regiment was the Rhodesian African Rifles (RAR). Led by white officers and NCOs the regiment was all black and every soldier was a volunteer. Highly respected, this regiment fought in Burma and Malaya and were also in Egypt during the Suez Crisis. Their regimental marching song was 'Sweet Banana' created, I believe, in 1942 when the RAR were sent to escort Italian POWs off ships arriving in Durban, South Africa. During the transition they stopped to buy bananas, abundant in Natal, which triggered the creation of 'Sweet Banana'.

There is a wonderful account of the RAR in Egypt when they were told their Commanding Officer was returning from home leave via the Suez Canal. Permission was given for every available man to be transported to the bank of the canal at the Farouk Cut and when the Durban Castle sailed past the CO took the salute from its bridge as the RAR's stirring chorus of 'Sweet Banana' filled the air.

'Sweet Banana' became a favourite with most Rhodesians during the bush war and I can remember as a teenager singing along to John Edmond's catchy version, my favourite bit being the drawn-out "Ba-nan-na, Ba-nan-na, I will buy you a Sweet Banana"!

I was 12 years old when the war started in 1964 so, really, I - and many others -knew nothing but war and international sanctions during our teenage years. We would listen to Sally Donaldson's Forces Requests every Saturday afternoon. She became 'the sweetheart of the nation', the equivalent of the UK's Vera Lynn, I suppose. We came to dread any TV or radio news reports beginning with "Combined Operations regret to advise ...." as well as news of casevacs (evacuation of casualties by air) as young men with horrifc and sometime fatal injuries were flown into the Andrew Fleming Hospital, the main hospital in Salisbury.

The reality of the war really set in after I had left school and was living at the Lady Stanley Girls Club. My first boyfriend was called-up for national service which meant six weeks in the bush and six weeks R&R (rest and recreation).

My younger brother, Bruce, was also called up at the same time so it was a double blow seeing them both off at the station. The comeraderie and cheefulness of the young men, I'm sure, belied their deeper fears. As the train pulled out of the station relatives and girlfriends tearfully waved them off, brave young boys who would become men overnight.

Life in the cities had its risks too which resulted in many whites, male and female, carrying weapons. Housewives carrying sub-machine guns became the norm as vigilance became a way of life, particularly when travelling out of the cities with the ever constant threat of terrorist ambushes. Mike - my future husband, who I introduce in a later chapter - was a territorial at the time, doing the 'six weeks in, six weeks out' stints. Whilst 'out' and back at work he was permitted to draw his G3 rifle and magazines from the Army Depot Armoury so that he could escort his boss to and from RISCO, the Rhodesian Iron and Steel Company, based in Redcliff near Que Que, just over 100 miles from Salisbury. His boss would be up front driving whilst Mike would be in the back seat 'riding shotgun'. I must admit, the image does makes me chuckle!

On roads deemed too dangerous convoys also became order of the day when travelling out of the city. Lines of 20 or so vehicles were escorted by the Police Reservists in heavily armed vehicles, usually Mazda pick-ups equipped with gun turrets and .03 Browning machine guns, riding up front, middle and behind. Anyone arriving too late to join the convoy would either have to make a dash to catch up with it or risk doing the journey on their own. Roads without convoys had Police warning signs erected on the outskirts of cities and towns advising motorists on long journeys not to travel after a certain time of day, normally 3 o'clock in the afternoon, as most ambushes occurred between then and dusk.

I recall a moment of madness when, after male problems, I decided 'come hell or high water' to get out of the city and spend the weekend with my close friend Cyn on the farm in Karoi, 114 miles from Salisbury. When I passed through Sinoia, about half way into the journey, it was exactly 3 o'clock and on the outskirts heading towards Karoi was a big sign warning folk not to travel after 3pm. As I had gone too far to turn back, it was a 'sh*t or bust' situation, leaving me with no option but to floor the pedal and hope and pray for the best! The conversation I jokingly had with Cyn prior to leaving Salisbury suddenly became a sickening reality - we agreed that if I didn't arrive in Karoi by a certain time she would alert the local 'stick' via the Agric-Alert (radio contact between farmers). A 'stick' was a quick response unit formed by farmers usually under the umbrella of the Police Anti-Terrorist Unit (PATU). As if things couldn't get any worse, I was in my brother's bright yellow Ford Escort, aptly knicknamed 'the banana' ...... an easy target if ever there was one!

Thankfully, I arrived safely in Karoi, relief overcoming me as I drove through the farm's security gates towards the farmhouse with its anti-grenade mesh at every window. All farmhouses were protected by security fences, either barbed or razor wire, and all farmers and their wives were armed with an assortment of weapons in which they and even their children were trained. I recall one weekend going with Cyn to visit her parents, Mr and Mrs B, on the farm in Karoi. Their security fence had bells attached to it which served as an early warning system as the slightest touch would set them off. One of the nights Mr B was away and it was just us girls, Cyn's mother and her brother Roy at home when we were awoken by the sound of the bells. Petrified Cyn and I huddled together in the double bed we shared as Roy slipped out into the darkness to investigate and Mrs B headed for the gun cabinet. The sight of Mrs B in her dressing gown and slippers standing in the bedroom doorway brandishing a huge weapon got both Cyn and I giggling nervously. Its funny what true nerves can do to you, but I knew for sure which scenario scared me the most ..... and it certainly wasn't the thought of gun-toting terrorists at the fence!! Thankfully, Roy returned confirming it was a false alarm and that the fence had been brushed by one of the farm animals.

That wasn't the only incident of Mrs B and a gun. Cyn tells the story when Roy called on Mr and Mrs B who were living in a small cottage on Roy's farm at the time. It was early evening and Mr and Mrs B were watching TV. After knocking several times and getting no response, in desperation he decided to throw stones onto the cottage's corrugated iron roof. The racket was almighty and, thinking they were under attack, Mrs B grabbed the gun while Mr B shouted "*shoot, shoot!*". So, there she was at the window in true 'Granny Clampett' style firing hell for leather, mainly up into the air which was more than lucky for Roy!

V

European Adventure

I n 1976 I left my job at Lange Menswear to go on a three months 'backpacking' trip to Europe with my best friend Cynthia. With Rhodesia still an unrecognised state and still under international sanctions there we very few countries that would accept us on Rhodesian passports, those being Spain - for which a visa was required - Switzerland and Greece. An example of the problems we encountered was flying via South Africa to Portugal which was also on our itinerary but, unbeknown to us - and, it seems our travel agent! - also required visas. It was only after arriving in Johannesburg for our connecting flight to Lisbon were we told about the visas. Although South African Airways, with a very good reputation to protect, were reluctant to fly us to Lisbon, after much deliberation they decided to take the risk. Not surprisingly, our arrival caused a real commotion with Cyn and I being taken to a little room where we sat awaiting our fate. Having never been out of Africa before we found the whole situation pretty daunting. Even the cleaners took an interest, with two rather large females stopping every so often to lean on their brooms and stare at us whilst animately whispering amongst themselves. After all the fuss and palarva we were surprised they agreed to let us into the country and even more surprised when they stamped our passports! Most countries were reluctant to stamp Rhodesian passports and would instead stamp a piece of paper which one carried in the passport. One thing that really bugged us was all the other young backpackers marvelling at the fact that, unlike them, we would fly from place to place rather than take trains across borders, which meant we were forever explaining how being Rhodesians restricted us enormously. Such were the joys of the travelling Rhodesian!

VI

The Whitsun Foundation

Following the three months trip to Europe I returned to Rhodesia and I took up a secretarial post with The Whitsun Foundation. The Foundation played a leading role in planning the development, mainly rural, of Rhodesia. It was inaugurated on 15 August 1975 as a non-profit development agency and funded by three major Rhodesian corporations, Shell, Delta Breweries and Tobacco Auction Holdings. Its objectives were preparing plans and projects, such as land reform, agricultural training colleges, small-scale rural industries, livestock management projects, rural family planning, rural afforstation, water development and suchlike for the development of the country, which could be funded by the International Bank for Reconstruction and Development (IBRD), or World Bank, and other international donors once UN sanctions were lifted and Rhodesia became Zimbabwe. Dr Ian Hume, a Rhodesian working for the World Bank, was invited to establish and run the Foundation. Our offices based in Shell House where, amusingly, the Shell employees treated us with great suspicion, referring to us as 'Kissinger's spies'! Mind you, if the truth be known, neither whites nor blacks trusted us, leaving us in a 'no win' situation all round. The 'Kissinger's spies' title came about around the time Henry Kissinger, the US Foreign Minister, met with the South African Prime Minister, John Vorster, in 1976 urging him to put pressure on Ian Smith to agree to a deal whereby majority rule would be put in place within two years. Ian Smith described this as a betrayal by South Africa, even writing a book about it, *'The Great Betrayal'*, especially as South Africa had assured Rhodesians they would not succumb to American pressure. Unfortunately, Rhodesia was totally dependent on South Africa, her only ally, and Rhodesians felt they had been sold-out with no alternative but to accept Kissinger's package, thereby majority rule becoming inevitable. Having accepted this, Rhodesians began to focus on a moderate black government rather than the communist-backed Mugabe and Nkomo thus, hopefully, ensuring the upkeep of lifestyle and standards Rhodesians had become accustomed to.

With the Foundation being treated with deep suspicion by ZANU-PF and their supporters, particularly where land reform was concerned, a number of the Foundation's pilot schemes in rural areas either came under threat or were attacked. Both in the cities and rural areas there was a climate of paranoia where everyone felt they were being watched and everywhere you looked posters screamed out *'Talk costs Lives'* etc etc. The Government constantly reminded us of the importance of remaining vigilant. We were told to be on our guard for suspicious packages or bags being left unattended, particularly after a bomb comprising of 34kg of TNT exploded in a branch of Woolworths in August 1977 killing 11 civilians, eight of which were black, and injurying 76. In December 1978 ZANLA forces bombed the Shell petrol storage depot in Salisbury, bringing the liberation struggle (bush war) to the capital. As a result, Shell House was on high alert. I recall an incident when, after entering the ladies toilets, I found an abandoned handbag. After checking the cubicles were empty I thought it best to err on the side of caution and report the incident to the Shell management. Before I knew what was happening sirens blared out as fire engines and police cars surrounded Shell House. Amidst the panic and confusion that ensued it was discovered the bag did, indeed, belong to one of Shell's employees. To make matters worse, though, one of the employees was that panicked she dashed to the loo to bring up and in so doing lost her false teeth down the pan! So, no guesses as to who was the most popular person in the building!

When Dr Hume returned to Washington his post was taken over by a retired Colonel, Don Grainger, a genteel, personable man. His loyalty to the Crown was well known and, indeed, his great friend was Sir Humphrey Gibbs, the former Governor of Rhodesia, who would often pop into the Foundation to pass the time of day over a cuppa with Colonel Grainger. I recall Sir Humphrey, a true gentleman, sitting in reception and feeling pity for this shadow of a man who had a defeated air about him. After UDI in 1965 Sir Humphrey, the last symbol of legality and loyalty to the Queen, became a virtual non-person, with mention of his name being blanked out and his residence, Government House, completely isolated.

VII

The Deafening Silence

By 1978 the nationalists - alliance of Mugabe's Zimbabwe African National Union (ZANU)/ZANLA Zim African National Lib Army and Nkomo's Zimbabwe African People's Union (ZAPU)/ZIPRA Zimbabwe People's Revolutionary Army, were becoming more effective. With white morale at an all time low with many feeling they were fighting a losing battle and the economy beginning to suffer, Ian Smith agreed to an 'Internal Settlement' with moderate colleague Bishop Abel Muzorewa which would end white minority rule and change the country's name to Zimbabwe-Rhodesia. With both Mugabe and Nkomo claiming Muzorewa a puppet of the white regime, plus the fact that Britain too refused to recognise the new order, the nationalists were spurred on even more. On 3 September 1978 Air Rhodesia flight 825 (Viscount Hunyani) on the last leg of its journey from Victoria Falls, via Kariba to Salisbury the capital, was shot down with a Soviet Strela 2 surface to air missile by insurgents of Nkomo's Zimbabwe People's Revolutionary Army (ZIPRA). Although the plane miraculously managed to land, it hit a ditch and broke up. Of the 52 passengers and four crew on board, 38 died and the insurgents, after having approached the wreckage, rounded up the 10 survivors they could see and shot them with automatic gunfire. Three passengers survived by hiding in the surrounding bush and a further five survived as they had gone to look for water at a nearby village before the insurgents arrived.

In retaliation for the shooting down of the civilian flight, Rhodesia Air Force Canberra Bombers, Hunter Fighter-Bombers and helicopter gunships attacked a terrorist base near Lusaka, warning Zambia by radio not to interfere. The commander of the raid was known as 'Green Leader'. Below is the taped conversation, courtesy The Mukiwa:

"Lusaka Tower, this is Green Leader. This is a message for the station commander at Mumba from the Rhodesian Air Force. We are attacking the terrorist base at Westlands farm at this time. This attack is against Rhodesian dissidents and not against Zambia. Rhodesia has no quarrel, repeat, no quarrel, with Zambia or her security forces. We therefore ask you not to intervene or oppose our attack. However, we are orbiting your airfield at this time and are under orders to shoot down any Zambian Air Force aircraft which does not comply with this request and attempts to take off. Did you copy all that?"

Lusaka Tower replies that they have understood and ask whether civil aircraft are still cleared to land. Green Leader asks them to wait half an hour or so. The impression given is very much that the Rhodesians are totally in control of the situation. And when Lusaka Tower was asked by the incoming Kenya

Airways jet who had priority, Lusaka Tower simply replied "I think the Rhodesians do".

Five months later an identical incident occurred when ZIPRA shot down a second Air Rhodesia Viscount (Unmiati) with 59 passengers and crew on board. There were no survivors.

The attacks were seen as acts of terrorism by the majority of Rhodesians, both black and white. With no condemnation from 'politically correct' overseas governments, in a sermon at a memorial service the Dean of the Anglican Church in Salisbury, Rev John da Costa, spoke of the 'deafening silence' of the international community.

VIII

End of the Bush War

Following the Internal Agreement, in late 1979 multiracial elections were held and won by Bishop Abel Muzorewa who replaced Ian Smith as Prime Minister in the newly-named Zimbabwe-Rhodesia. Muzorewa's new government, however, failed to win international recognition and with neither side in the war achieving military victory, negotiations between the Government of Zimbabwe-Rhodesia, the UK Government and Mugabe and Nkomo's united Patriotic Front took place at Lancaster House, London in 1979 where the Lancaster House Agreement of December 1979 was signed which formally ended the Bush War, temporarily placing Rhodesia back under the control of Britain while fresh elections were organised. The last British Governor of Rhodesia during this short period was Lord Christopher Soames. With a ceasefire implemented, some 1500 Commonwealth Monitoring Force peacekeepers and observers from Britain, Australia, Fiji, Kenya and New Zealand arrived to oversee the operation. The CMF played a vital role in peacekeeping between the guerillas and Rhodesian forces. 16 assembly areas spread throughout the country received some 22,000 guerillas whose names and weapons were registered. During the elections British police were observers at polling stations. Although the elections were about giving the blacks a free and fair vote many wanting to vote for Ian Smith were barred by the Lancaster House Agreement resulting in a two-horse race as Mugabe and Nkomo jostled for power. During these elections Mugabe's ZANU-PF election symbol was a crowing cockerel set against a rising sun. '*The cockerel of liberation*' was an image which identified with the masses, the majority of whom were peasant farmers. Mugabe won a landslide victory and the new government was put in place with Mugabe becoming Prime Minister of the Republic of Zimbabwe and Canaan Banana President. This gave rise to the joke being bandied around *"we were promised a cock and all we got was a banana"*!

With no safeguards for the white minority, many of whom were third or fourth generation, and the fear of retribution from the new government many whites began to emigrate, mainly by road via the border at Beit Bridge into South Africa. This route became known as 'taking the gap' or the 'Chicken Run' by resolute remaining whites, many of whom were 'financial prisoners' who decided to stick it out in the hopes that things wouldn't be as bad as they had anticipated and, indeed, in his inauguration speech Mugabe appealed to whites to remain in the country and build a nation based on national unity which the whites, and farmers in particular, gratefully accepted.

With the faction-ridden nature of Zimbabwean politics, in 1983, barely three years after independence, Mugabe's true colours came to light after he ordered his fearsome North Korean-trained 5th Brigade to launch Operation Gukurahundi, *the early rains that wash away the chaff,* in the southern province of Matabeleland, killing around 20,000 Ndebele civilians, most of whom were supporters of Joshua Nkomo's ZAPU party, a massacre even Mugabe later referred to as 'a moment of madness'. These 'dissidents' were forced to dig their own graves and their wives and children were forced not only to bury them alive, but dance on top of their graves. People, including women and children, were being gunned down or herded into huts which were set alight, the soldiers outside warning that any of them attempting to escape would be shot. International condemnation was non-existent, dangerously giving Mugabe a licence to kill. In 1987, a defeated Joshua Nkomo, the father of black Zimbabwean nationalism, was coerced by Mugabe into a 'Unity Accord', which effectively created a one-party state with Mugabe as its leader and, as the saying goes, the rest is history......

IX

Mike

Turning into the driveway to Hillcrest, the home of a good friend's mother-in-law, Mrs Dee, I had no reason to suspect anything was untoward. Out of the blue she had invited me to dinner which I didn't think unusual as she was well-known for her dinner parties. As I bumped along the dirt road leading up to the house, which looked welcoming with brightly coloured lights along the front, I began to wonder who else would be there. Reaching the crest I got out of the car and was greeted at the door by Mrs Dee and Shandy her Rhodesian Ridgeback. Curiously I looked beyond her and could see only one other person. It was Mike, one of her lodgers. With introductions over I looked towards the dining table and noticed only three place settings. Great! I thought, my heart slowly sinking. By this time I was beginning to feel extremely uncomfortable. Both Mike and I took an instant dislike to one another. For me, not only was it his shoulder-length hair which put me off, but also the medallion hanging around his neck which, to this day, he swears was his cherished gold ingot!

Mike thought I was too uptight, which wasn't surprising considering the circumstances! I was surprised when towards the end of the evening Mike asked me out the following evening, a Wednesday. Without hesitation I told him I was playing squash. He then mentioned Thursday evening and I, again, responded promptly saying it was my gym evening. Inwardly sighing with relief I really thought I had got myself out of a couple of tight spots! So you can imagine my surprise when he pushed further and asked about Friday evening! I can't remember my excuse, but by the time he had got to Saturday the excuses had run dry!

So Saturday it was. Little did either of us know then that this would be the beginning of a lifetime of the 'irresistible force meeting the immovable object'!

Having never heard a 'Brummie' accent, the 'twang' in Mike's accent made me think he was Australian. I learned he was born in Birmingham in the UK and at the beginning of 1969 whilst working for Lucas Engineering he was offered the opportunity of a two-year contract in South Africa, which he eagerly accepted. After 20 months in Johannesburg he decided to return to the UK but before heading home he thought he'd pay a quick visit north of the border to see the 'rebels' in Rhodesia. As a British passport holder he approached the border at Beit Bridge in trepidation. After all, in 1965 whilst watching the TV when Ian Smith declared the Unilateral Declaration of Independence (UDI) he recalls saying to himself "*Send in the troops, how dare they rebel against the Queen!"*, not realising five years later he would not only be standing on the Rhodesian border but also becoming a territorial in the Rhodesian Army! After crossing the border he was amazed at how different the atmosphere in Rhodesia was to that in South Africa and how friendly and cheerful the people were, whites and blacks. He fell in love with the country and what was supposed to be a very quick two week visit lasted 17 years!

X

Cerebral Malaria

Mike and I had spent Christmas 1982 with Cyn and her family on the farm in Karoi. Roughly ten days later I began to feel extremely unwell, with an excruciating headache, aching joints and weakness at the knees. Our local chemist, and African man, took one look at me supporting myself on the counter and said without hesitation "*You have malaria*" and urged me to get to the doctor as soon as possible. I suspected he could be right with Karoi's close proximity to the Zambezi escarpment, a high-risk malaria area, particularly during December's heavy rains. Growing up and, indeed, as an adult I had never taken malaria tablets, even when venturing out of the city, so it was just a case of bad luck being bitten by a malaria-carrying mozzie! I believe not all mosquitos carry malaria, only the female Anopheles. Unlike other mosquitos, these are silent meaning one is totally unaware of their presence. Apparently, if one does hear mosquitos buzzing then there's no need to worry. How true this is, I'm not sure, but as far as I am concerned the only good mozzie is a dead one, silent assassin or not!

I managed to get an emergency appointment at the doctor's where blood tests were done. The surgery, like my flat, was in 'the Avenues' a short walk away. How I managed to walk there and back home is anyone's guess. Barely through the door of my flat, feverish and weak, I made a beeline for the fridge. Grabbing an ice-cold bottle of water I frantically began to drink, water overflowing onto the floor, in a desperate attempt to quench my insatiable thirst. Amidst all this the phone began to ring. Making my way out of the kitchen I picked it up, by which time I was retching, bringing back up all the liquid I had just consumed. The voice on the other end was the receptionist at the doctor's surgery with the results of the blood tests. It was cerebral malaria (Plasmodium Falciparum malaria). She stressed I needed to get to hospital as soon as possible and asked for Mike's contact details. Between convulsive bouts of vomiting I managed to give her Mike's work number and when he arrived home he rushed me through to the Parirenyatwa, Harare's main hospital, where we were met by my doctor and a specialist in tropical diseases. I was immediately put on an intravenous quinine drip and placed in a ward with three other patients, all African women, whose emaciated bodies lay motionless on sweat-soaked sheets. Time is of the essence when dealing with cerebral malaria as it can cause brain damage or slipping into a coma. It has a very high mortality rate and although more dangerous than the normal recurring malaria, if you're lucky enough to survive cerebral malaria, there is no chance of relapse as it does not have a latent stage in the body and, for that, I was at least thankful!

I'm not sure how long I lay there. I vaguely remember Mike coming and going and the Pastor of our church and his wife praying over me. Unable to get my temperature down the hospital asked Mike to bring in an electric fan which did the job but with me subsequently ending up with pneumonia! When I eventually left the hospital the fan, which Mike had borrowed from a friend, was nowhere to be seen and we can only assume one of the nursing staff must have taken a shine to it!

It was while I was in hospital Mike organised our wedding, a small affair attended by about 40 family and friends which was held in our favourite restaurant, Tavern Bacchus. Actually, the restaurant was a favourite haunt of Mike's long before I had met him. Apparently, he did all his dating at Tavern Bacchus and it was after taking me there a second time the owner, Joan, said to him "*When you brought Sheila here a second time I knew your number was up!*".

We honeymooned at the A'zambezi River Lodge, a beautiful setting on the banks of the Zambezi River, about four miles from the stunning Victoria Falls. Lunch was usually a braai (BBQ) set up in the gardens close to the swimming pool. Every day at noon on the dot rolls and salads would be laid out in readiness for lunch. It was on our first day whilst relaxing by the pool when suddenly the peace was shattered and the air was filled with high pitched screeching and chitter-chatter. The trees along the water's edge began to rustle and sway as a horde of vervet monkeys swung their way towards the laden table where they grabbed every roll in sight before dashing away again up into the trees. Thieving wasn't just at lunch time, as I was to later discover after ordering a 'Ginger Square', a popular refreshing drink. The drink came decorated with a slice of orange and, even though normally timid creatures, the monkeys would brave coming really close and, with their eyes fixed steadfastly on me, one hand would hold the glass whilst the other dislodged the slice of orange! Not once did they spill the drink and fascinated by their dexterity, not to mention cheekiness, this became a daily ritual which I actually began to look forward to!

Evening meals were in the Lodge's restaurant and it was here Mike tried crocodile tail for the first time! Even though it looked very much like chicken I wasn't having any of it and even shudder at the thought now!

Of course, a trip to the Falls, one of the seven natural wonders of the world, was a must, as was a walk through the 'rain forest', a constant fine spray from the flow of the Falls. Situated between Zambia and Zimbabwe each country has a different view. Although Zimbabwe has the amazing panoramic views, Zambia has the adrenalin addict's Devil's Pool which can be accessed from the Zimbabwe side. The Pool and many other smaller rock pools on the top of the Falls were the result of thousands of years of erosion. Known as the 'ultimate infinity pool', Devil's Pool sits at the very edge of the Falls, with its rock lip being the only protection from tipping over the edge.

Victoria Falls

Today, there is talk of renaming Victoria Falls, named after Queen Victoria, Mosi oa Tunya '*the smoke that thunders*'.

XI

Easther

Where do I begin with Easther? Pronounced '*Esther*', I often wondered whether the spelling of her name was more 'lost in translation', a common trait with many locals taking on colonial names. Conversations, too, were often 'lost' this way, a prime example being "Did you walk or ride your bicycle to the shops?" to which the reply would be "Yes" and one would then have to ask "Yes, what? Walk or ride?".

At just a slip of a girl she worked as a domestic for Mike and his first wife. When Mike bought the marital home Easther came with it so, I suppose, you could say he 'inherited' her. He sent her on various cookery courses and she not only became proficient in cooking but also knowledgable about social etiquette and wasn't daunted by laying a table for dinner parties.

Easther left Mike's employ when he got divorced and went into lodgings. She always kept in touch with him though in the hopes that one day she would be able to work for him again. When she heard Mike and I were getting married she sought him out and begged for a job. I was a little hesitant but with Easther's persistence and Mike's cajoling I eventually succumbed and we took her on in January 1983. Shortly after we got married we moved from my little flat in the Avenues to a garden flat in Avondale, a suburb on the outskirts of Harare. Easther was thrilled as it meant her having her own accommodation and not having the lengthy daily commute from the township on the other side of town. Her kaya, situated at the back of the property, consisted of a bedroom/sitting room and an ablution/washing-up area.

The day we moved was extremely hot which took its toll on the chicken I had bought for our evening meal. By the time we'd come to cook it we found it had gone rancid. The smell was putrid to say the least and after hastily wrapping it back up Mike went out the back and threw it in the rubbish bin. About five minutes later he had reason to go to the bin again and found the chicken missing! We suspected Easther had quickly rushed out and retrieved it for her pot. We never mentioned it to her, but thanked God she had a strong constitution!

Although married herself, Easther didn't see much of her husband, Boniface, who was a long-distance lorry driver. Like Easther, Boniface was always cheerful and polite. When he did visit he always made a point of coming over to say hello to us. They were childless which we thought quite strange, particularly as children are highly prized and play a big part in African culture.

Easther looked after us and we looked after her. She cleaned, cooked and did our washing and ironing. She would pop out to do our day-to-day grocery shopping at the local supermarket a short walk away, something she always looked forward to as it gave her an opportunity to socialise and catch up with other domestics in the area. We were always in awe at how adept she was in balancing a box of groceries on her head, arms swaying at her sides. Carrying wares on their heads is a common practice. Zimbabweans have an amazing sense of balance and it's not uncommon to see them haphazardly carrying all sorts of things on their heads or precariously on bicyles!

During her breaks Easther would sit on the grassy verge beside the road chatting to friends. Very hot days would see the group huddling together under brightly coloured umbrellas from which emanated high pitched chatter and raucous laughter.

As well as paying her a wage we also subsidised her food, a common practice with most domestic workers. As well as mealie meal (sadza), the staple diet, we also subsidised her meat. Easther would accompany us to the butcher's once a month to stock up in bulk, her choice always being the cheaper cuts with loads of bones which she would make into a tasty stew to accompany the rather bland sadza. Shopping in bulk was not a normal practice for her but as we had more than enough freezer space we gave her sole use of the freezer above the fridge. She was probably the only domestic in the area or, indeed, Harare to have her own freezer!

With a varied repertoire of tasty meals to prepare, Easther could never understand Mike's passion for chips which he had with virtually every meal, resulting in her nicknaming him 'Mr Chips'. Another thing that flummoxed her was our love of plain and simple baked beans on toast and amused us with her pronounciation of 'buggered' beans on toast, a term Mike and I still use to this day!

Although a year or so younger than me, Easther had a child-like mentality. There were things she just couldn't comprehend. When pointing to the moon and telling her that man actually walked on it, aghast she replied *"aikhona (no way!), it is too small!"*, shaking her head and laughing out loud at my stupidity!

When Mike and I flew to Bulawayo, Zimbabwe's second city, to visit our good friends John and Cyn Pybus, we decided to take Easther along too. She knew Sylvia, the Pybus's domestic and we thought it would be good for them to get together. Not only that, we also thought it would give Easther a once in a lifetime opportunity. If she didn't have any concept of the size of the moon, she certainly didn't have any concept of flying!

On the day of the flight Easther, with child-like excitement, had her bag packed hours before we left for the airport. Dressed 'to the nines' she made Mike and I look like the poor relations in our denims and T-shirts!

Like a duck to water she took it all in her stride, not even flinching on take-off. Not long into the flight she asked if she could open the window. Curious as to why she couldn't, and after our failed attempts in explaining why, realisation suddenly crossed her face after droplets of condensation began to drip from the air vent above her head "*Aah, it is raining, that's why we cannot open the window!*"

Like all 'second' cities Bulawayo was always the bridesmaid and never the bride. Salisbury (Harare), the capital, considered the 'in' place and where everything happened became known by Bulawayians as 'Bamba Zonke', meaning '*grab the lot*'. That said, Bulawayo was special in her own way. Her streets, laid out in 1894, were decreed by Cecil John Rhodes to forever be wide enough for a full span of 16 oxen to turn in, and so they still are.

Bulawayo's main claim to fame, however, lies just 35kms south east of the city in the Matopo Hills and Matobo National Park, a UNESCO World Heritage Site. The site of granite kopjes, or small hills, is landscaped with numerous boulders which the Ndebele warrior king, Mzilikazi, father of Lobengula, named 'Matobo', the Matabele word for 'bald-headed'.

It is here at the top of one of the Matobo rocks at 'World's View' where Cecil John Rhodes is buried. Rhodes once visited the place and was so taken with it he requested he be buried there, a burial which was attended by Ndbele chiefs who, for the first time ever, afforded a white man the Matabele royal salute 'Bayete', meaning 'exalted king'. It is also here where Mzilikazi and Lobengula are buried.

Here lie the remains of Cecil John Rhodes

In recent years the war veterans have pushed for Rhodes' body to be exhumed and his remains returned to the UK, blaming them for the lack of rain in the area. But Mugabe blocked their plans saying *"his legacy is part of the country's national history and heritage"* and that *"the grave was an important reminder of the country's colonialist past which could not be airbrushed out"*.

The site still attracts thousands of visitors each year, bringing much needed revenue to the area. In years gone by an added attraction was the 'Lizard Man', an elderly local known as the 'Pied Piper of lizards' who used to speak to the rainbow lizards - named as such due to their mixed colourings of blue, green, yellow and red - summoning them to him to be fed.

Always very shrewd with money Easther became our 'bank' most Friday evenings when we fancied a meal out. Unable to get to the bank during the day we would borrow cash for a meal and repay our debt on the Saturday. We expressed our concern at the amount of cash Easther stashed away in her kaya and suggested her accompanying us to the bank one Saturday morning to open her own bank account, which she did.

We trusted Easther implicitly. Whenever we were away she would keep an eye on the property, every evening drawing the curtains and switching on the lights. No-one would ever guess the property was unoccupied. Most evenings she would settle down in the lounge to watch the TV before closing-up for the night. On the two occasions we holidayed in the UK shortly before leaving Africa we always ensured we returned with presents for both Easther and Boniface. Watches were always popular and, of course, umbrellas. I was surprised when Easther reciprocated. On her annual two-week holiday Easther would invariably go home to Mtoko, her village some 90 miles away, but occasionally she would travel by train to Botswana. Shopping trips across the border were common with the locals who would buy cheap items to bring back to re-sell in Zimbabwe. After one of these trips she presented me with a little parcel crudely wrapped in newspaper. Her face beamed with childlike anticipation as she willed me to unwrap the gift there and then. Her excitement was infectious and I hurriedly tore away the paper revealing plastic roses in various colours - blue, green and purple -

standing proud in a white plastic swan. She knew I liked to pick roses from the garden and display them on the mantelpiece and said *"I know you love roses and these will never die"*. Garish as they were I was truly touched and put the ornament on the mantelpiece where it remained until we left Africa when I returned it to Easther requesting she take good care of it. It thrilled her to know that something which had taken pride of place on our mantelpiece was now going to be displayed in her kaya!

XII

UK Bound

By 1986, after living under Mugabe's one party state for six years, we began to see 'the writing on the wall'. That same year the Presidential Powers Act had been passed, supposedly a 'temporary measure' giving Mugabe the power to change any law at will and, after much deliberation, Mike and I decided to leave Zimbabwe to settle in the UK. The final nail in the coffin, at least for Mike, was when Mugabe decided to abolish dual-citizenship, meaning if we stayed Mike would have to relinquish his British passport, something he was not prepared to do and I didn't blame him!

Other laws that affected us were the ones Mugabe hurriedly passed shortly after taking power, one being emigrants restricted to taking no more than a couple of hundred Zimbabwe dollars with them and the other restricting emigrants from taking household furniture less three years old. Most, if not all, of our furniture was virtually brand new which meant we had to leave the lot behind which was subsequently shared amongst friends. Mike also lost his paid-up Prudential pension and two life insurance policies when the Pru sold out to a local insurance company. So, we left Zimbabwe virtually penniless.

Saying goodbye to family and friends was painful, but none more so than saying goodbye to Easther who we considered very much part of our family. My last image of Easther was of her standing at the kitchen sink where she was doing the last bits of the day's washing-up. *"Go, you must go now"* she said turning her head away from me. I walked out the door and wept.

We were able to correspond with Easther but had to keep our letters very simple. Although she had very limited English and writing skills we were, thankfully, able to get the gist of what she was saying and were thrilled to read in one of her letters our good friend and ex-neighbour, Jenny, had taken her on. To know she was still in employment was a great relief, particularly as we desparately tried to find her a new employer before leaving Zimbabwe.

Our trips back to Zimbabwe always saw us seeking Easther out. Our first reunion, after 10 years in 1996, was a joyous one. To mark the occasion we lined up for a photo. Easther who, for one moment was standing between Mike and I, suddenly disappeared. After looking around and then down I saw she was kneeling. *"Get up Easther!"* I urged but she just looked up at me and said *"You are my parents, that is why I must kneel"*. In her culture kneeling shows respect, particularly for elders and parents.

We saw Easther again a couple of years later in 1998, little knowing it would be the last time. She was still working for Jenny who had left the garden flat and moved into a house a little further out of town. The meeting, as usual, was filled with joy and laughter and when we got into the car to leave she surprised us by promptly opening the back door and settling comfortably on the back seat. Mike and I looked quizzically at one another before she excitedly said "*I want to take you to see my house*". Before we left Africa we gave Easther money to build her own house. As we drove along the makeshift bumpy road in the township of Chitungwiza we were aware of the interest we generated, with curious eyes peering through the windows at us. Driving deep into the township wasn't really an area for whites which we found a little unnerving, but with Easther in the back we somehow felt reassured. We eventually reached her house which, like all the others surrounding it, was very basic. Easther stood proudly at the door whilst we took a photo and after a rushed tour we quickly made our escape.

When Jenny left Africa we didn't know what became of Easther. After trying to contact her without much luck we asked our close friend Cyn to make enquiries as to her whereabouts.

Coincidentally, around about that time I was watching a BBC news report regarding allegations made in 2011 that a third of registered voters in Zimbabwe were actually dead. Close up footage of an open page of the death register was briefly shown and one name – Easther – jumped out at me, leaving me with a sense of foreboding as there was only one person I knew who spelt her name that way. Not long after that report and following enquiries on the ground in Zimbabwe Cyn contacted us in 2012 with news that Easther, sadly, had died a couple of years earlier. Sadness overwhelmed me and to this day I still wish I had kept those plastic roses.

Part 2

Reunion

ive years on and I am, again, homeward bound to my beloved Zimbabwe, this time flying from Birmingham International on Emirates via Dubai. A roundabout route, I know, but very few airlines fly to Zimbabwe and Kenya Airways, a more direct flight, was fully booked.

I'm on my way to a reunion of some of the girls I grew up with in the Rhodesia Children's Home. It must be 50 years or so since last I saw them. Some of the girls still live in Zimbabwe, whilst others are travelling from further afield - Cathy and her husband, Neil, from Australia and Betty, like me, from the UK. As Betty is flying from Heathrow to Dubai we shall be meeting up in Dubai before flying the eight hour journey, via Lusaka, to Harare. I fondly remember Betty as the girl who mistook me for her sister Wilma when I first arrived at the Home in 1960. I joked she may not recognise me now, to which she replied "*Oh, I will*".

There were a lot of spare seats on the flight and I ended up with three to myself meaning I could spread out and at least get a bit of shut-eye before arriving in Dubai. I had heard Dubai was a massive airport and, given the fact not only was I travelling on my own but also my stop-over was only one hour five minutes long, I began to panic that I would miss my connecting flight onto Harare. As if time wasn't short enough, I couldn't believe it when upon arriving in Dubai and taxi-ing along the runway to our jet bridge the plane suddenly came to a halt and the pilot said we would have to wait as another plane was still being loaded at our bridge. The fifteen minutes or so we sat on the runway seemed like an eternity and when we eventually got to the bridge and the plane came to a stop I rushed down the aisle apologizing as I went explaining I had a connecting flight to which one lady replied *"Well, we all do"*. When I told her how limited I was time-wise she actually began to panic for me! How I made my connecting flight I shall never know. Looking around in desperation I asked a very kind young man who, unbeknown to me had also been on the Birmingham to Dubai flight, for help. As he had time to kill he offered to see me right to my gate. After walking for what seemed like miles, taking a couple of lifts and a tube-like train, I finally made it to the gate. Thanking the young man I dashed towards a packed lift where the attendant was calling out *"Anyone for Lusaka or Harare?"* to which I breathlessly replied *"Yes, me!!"*. As I got in I sighed with relief as I knew Betty would be worrying herself sick I wasn't going to make it. Betty had assisted travel and, unbeknown to me, was waiting with her attendant near the lift when she saw me dash past. *"There she is, follow her!!"* she shouted excitedly. I was barely in the lift when this wheelchair virtually rammed up my behind with Betty excitedly calling my name. I turned round and saw her and we hugged each other, laughing all the while, totally oblivious of the jam-packed lift. Our laughter was infectious and soon the whole lift laughed along with us as they shared our joy, unaware they were witnessing the reunion of two old friends who hadn't seen each other in 50 years! Once out of the lift we boarded a bus to take us to the plane. We had separate seats and after settling in I began to think of Betty and wonder whether life had been kind to her after leaving the Home. She was born in Scotland and was extremely close to her dad who used to visit her regularly. When his visits suddenly stopped and after three weeks of hearing nothing both Betty and Mrs Whittall, the Head Matron, knew something was seriously amiss. It was Mrs Whittall who found out Betty's dad was in the Belgian Congo as a mercenary. Shortly after this discovery Betty got a letter from him from the Congo explaining he couldn't come to say goodbye because if he had he knew he would never leave and he promised he would make enough money and return to take Betty and her two sisters back to Scotland. After that first letter Betty received two more saying he was well and was looking forward to seeing her soon.

One night a group of us girls, excluding Betty, were watching the news on TV when a report came in saying the first Rhodesian mercenary had been killed in the Congo and our instant reaction was *"Oh no, please don't let it be Betty's dad"*. No name was given at the time and we all made a pact not to say anything to Betty and have her worry unnessarily. The following morning at 6 o'clock Mrs Whittall arrived in Davies House, one of the five 'houses' which made up the Home. We all thought it strange as she hardly ever visited the houses, let alone at 6 o'clock in the morning. It was only when we heard Auntie Bessie, our House Matron, call Betty that a sense of foreboding overcame us. Betty was in the bath at the time and automatically thought *"what have I done now?"*. Jumping out of the bath she ran to Auntie Bessie's room where Mrs Whittall sat holding a newspaper. *"It's my dad, isn't it, is he hurt?"* to which Mrs Whittall replied *"I'm very sorry Betty"* before showing her the newspaper. Overcome with grief Betty collapsed. Today she recalls how we girls wept with her, surrounding her with love and support. The Congolese Government paid out a large amount to Betty who, by then, was the only one of the family left in the Home, her sisters having been adopted into very comfortable homes. Although no amount of money could compensate for the loss of her beloved dad the money was put to good use and, at the suggestion of the Home, Betty was enrolled in Marymount, a prestigious Catholic-run school in Umtali in Rhodesia's Eastern Highlands where she spent two years, followed by a Musgrove & Watson tour of Europe. The remainder of the money was controlled by the Master of the High Court but Betty never went short.

Today she is happily married with a daughter and grand-daughter, both of whom she absolutely adores, as they do her.

I have my trusty camera with me on the flight as we'll be travelling through the day from Dubai to Harare and I love to photograph Africa from the air. Unlike my previous visit back in 2013, this time I will have to be more cautious where taking photos is concerned. Travellers to Zimbabwe are warned not to take photos of strategic facilities, such as airports, or sensitive places, such as presidential or diplomatic residences. I remember in 2013 revisiting the garden flat in Avondale Mike and I lived in prior to leaving Zimbabwe. As it had changed so much I was keen to take a photo to show Mike upon my return to the UK. Now a business it was virtually unrecognisable. I felt it only polite to go in and ask permission to photograph the flat from the road. I was treated with great suspicion with the owner asking if I was from the BBC! I told him I wasn't and whilst in Reception I began to describe the layout of the place as it was when Mike and I lived there. That seemed to do the trick and amidst his grunting and still suspicious look I left to take photos from the road.

Well into the flight and after lunch I settled back in my seat, gazing down on a barren brown canvas as, come September, Africa emerges from winter into summer, bringing with it much needed rain. My thoughts turn to what changes, if any, we'd find on our arrival in Zimbabwe, particularly following the recent elections in July.

These elections saw many hoping real change would come to this beleagured nation. Sadly though, amid accusations of vote rigging, ZANU(PF) regained power, with Emmerson Mnangagwa, dubbed 'the crocodile', becoming President, a man whose police force, post the 2018 elections, hounded and took away the opposition for questioning and whose army inflicted brutal attacks on people outside Harare during which six people were killed. Worryingly, Mnangagwa as Minister of State Security under Mugabe's rule played a crucial role in Operation Gukurahundi, the ethnic cleansing by Mugabe's North Korean-trained Fifth Brigade of some 20,000 Ndebele people. With the new President being a carbon copy of the old one I am keen to see what changes, if any, there are on touch-down at Robert Gabriel Mugabe International Airport.

Looking out the window as we entered Zimbabwe I was shocked to see numerous bush fires and huge patches of black scorched earth blotting the landscape. I remembered fires like this in my childhood, which were normal just before the rains, but they certainly were never on a massive scale such as this. Curiosity getting the better of me I made a mental note to ask the reason behind such destruction.

After landing in Harare, being on British passports, Betty and I had to obtain visas at a cost of US$55 each. The officer we dealt with was extremely pleasant and helpful, even lending me his pen to fill in the necessary form. Unfortunately, the pen had seen better days and I was mortified when attempting to write with it I split the case from the nib upwards. His face fell and I apologized profusely, however his whole expression and demeanour changed in an instant when Betty pulled out a brand spanking new shiny pen from her bag and gave it to him!

It was great being reunited with John and Cyn again and before leaving the airport Cyn and I dashed to the loo. She disappeared into a cubicle and I dashed into the next. Oh, the relief! I was still in full flow when Cyn emerged from her cubicle, coming face-to-face with a line of urinals. *"We're in the men's toilets!"* she shrieked. The exhilaration of relief turned to panic as I desparately tried to switch off midstream. Adjusting myself as best I could and amidst raucous laughter we fled the scene, hurrying to catch up with John and Betty.

Getting out of the airport was somewhat chaotic and the ride home to John and Cyn's was a bit of a nightmare as we tried to negotiate the rush hour traffic. A lot of drivers just seem to do their own thing, many going through red lights willy-nilly, including hoards of taxis for the locals, jam-packed with passengers all keen to make their way home. As soon as the security gate rolled closed behind us at John and Cyn's the chaos of the rush hour was replaced by serenity. After getting out of the car we were met by Doreen, Cynthia's domestic. I had only expected to see her in the morning and had practised my Shona, the local language, to greet her. So, '*Makadiyi*', "*how are you?*" said to someone you haven't seen in a long time became the boring bog standard "*Hello Doreen, good to see you!*" as we hugged. I made up for it the next morning, however, by greeting her with "*Mangwanani, mamuka sei*", "*Good Morning, how are you?*, a greeting she taught me on my last visit in 2013. Zimbabwe has 16 official languages, the most in the world, with the most widely spoken being Shona, Ndebele and English. Shona, a Bantu language, is native to the Shona tribe, people who reside in Mashonaland (Harare area) and Ndebele is native to the Matebele tribe who reside in Matabeleland (Bulawayo area).

As dusk fell we sat outside with sundowners and I re-acquainted myself with the beautiful garden as well as Rover and Buffy the dogs and, of couse, the boss of the house, Biggles the African Grey parrot. Later, we were joined by two more friends, Cathy, who had also just arrived in Zimbabwe with her husband Neil and Betsy who now lives in Harare. Again, it had been 50 years since last I saw Cathy and Betsy, both of whom were also in the Rhodesia Children's Home. The common denominator for the three of us was coming from families ruined by alcohol. I was pleased to see that life had been good to Cathy. It was lovely meeting Neil her husband, a New Zealander, who I had heard so much about from Betty. He and Cathy now live in Australia and have two sons and one grandson, the apple of their eye. Betsy's life, too, was good. Having lived in Bulawayo, Mozambique and, finally, Swaziland, Betsy returned to Zimbabwe after her beloved husband, Bruce, passed away. Today she lives in Harare with her daughter, Lisa, Lisa's partner Mario, and two beautiful grandchildren, Tyler and Bryony-Rose. Not being, in her words, 'a people person' she lives separately in a lovely little cottage on the property with her two beloved

Jack Russells, Hannah and Rusty. I was pleased to have the opportunity of telling Betsy what an influence she had on me whilst in the Home. An avid reader, her general knowledge was second to none and I remember looking up to her and thinking she was one of the cleverest people I'd ever known!

After our brief get-together at Cyn and John's we all decided to meet for coffee the following morning. On the way to the meet-up we were suddenly stopped at traffic lights by the sound of sirens and the outriders of President Mnangagwa's cavalcade. Stopping momentarily right in the middle of the intersection the outriders quickly made off again, a line of official looking vehicles in their wake followed by Mnangagwa's limosine which, in turn, was followed by a heavily armed troop carrier and small ambulance at the rear. It reminded me of when, back in 2013, I stood at the roadside watching Mugabe's cavalcade go by and I realise nothing much has changed. During the Mugabe era the cavalcade was known as 'Bob and his Wailers', the name arising following Bob Marley and his Wailers playing at Zimbabwe's independence celebrations in 1980.

We finally got to the cafe where over coffee Cathy handed round black and white photos from when we were in the Home. How we laughed at ourselves back then! What poor Neil must have thought sitting amongst all these women, is anyone's guess!

That afternoon, at Betty's request, John took us to Royal Harare Golf Club. Betty's first husband, Glen, was a very keen golfer and Betty remembers spending many a happy time at the Club. Reminiscing she said the Club House hadn't changed a bit. We took a walk alongside the fairway under the shade of Acacia and Msasa trees. As we approached a bunker we saw a lone duiker (small buck) and were told these timid little creatures roam the golf course. After having tea on the balcony overlooking the course and just before the sun began to set we made for home.

Our reunion lunch the following day was held at Spring Fever, a well-known and reputable restaurant on the outskirts of Harare. There were 11 of us and we sat down to a three course meal. It was a happy event filled with memories and laughter. Before going our separate ways Neil, Cathy, Betty and I arranged to visit the Home the next day. I was looking forward to seeing Precious, the young girl I sponsored back in 2013, again and after arriving at the Home was thrilled when the matron in charge suggested Precious - who had been taken on by the Home as their seamstress/mender following her sewing course in 2013 - show us around. Our reunion was joyful as we hugged each other and I was surprised to learn Precious was now married and expecting a baby!

Sadly, things had gone downhill somewhat since my last visit. The high cost of electricity rendered the huge stoves in the kitchen redundant, a problem resolved by erecting a makeshift kitchen in the children's playground which consisted of a corrugated roof supported on wooden poles. At the time of our visit it was nearing lunchtime and large black pots of sadza (maize meal) and nyama (meat) bubbled away on open fires. Other victims to economic restraint were the on-site clinic, the building now being rented for boarding accommodation by Roosevelt Girls High School a short walk away and the two huge washing machines in the laundry which now stand idle awaiting much needed spare parts. All washing is now done by hand, no mean feat with a hundred or so children to cater for. One positive was the continued availability of hot water following the installation of solar panels.

Other forms of desparately needed revenue are the little conference centre, built since last I visited, which is rented out for meetings, parties and even weddings and also the thriving vegetable plot providing primarily for the children with any surpluses being sold on.

The following day, Tuesday, we left Harare for Lake Kariba, meeting up with Neil and Cathy along the way. At 5.15a.m. it was still dark but we had to make an early start for the five to six hour journey to Kariba in order to set sail mid-day ensuring we reached our first mooring before nightfall. Along the way I saw close-up the vast areas of scorched blackened earth, literally a 'scorched earth policy', which seemed to go on for miles and when I asked Cyn about them she replied many are started deliberately by the locals, making it easier for them to dig for rats, not only because rats are a part of their diet, but also because of the chronic food shortages. As on my last visit in 2013 most barns and grain silos still stand empty following the land invasions in 2000 which saw white farmers driven off their farms.

We did our usual stop at the small town of Lion's Den for breakfast, with a choice of steak or boerewors (spicey sausage) rolls and fried onions accompanied by a large cup of tea. We sat in the luscious green garden on exquisite furniture, long wooden benches and tables made from the Mawanga tree, prolific in the area. After breakfast we stocked up on biltong (air-dried beef) before heading on our journey north. I was amazed at how busy the road to Kariba was. Known as the Harare-Chirundu Highway it is part of the North-South Corridor (Cairo-Cape Town Highway) used by haulage trucks carrying heavy loads of brand new plant and machinery from South Africa to Zambia, Tanzania and onwards.

African Huts

One thing that never fails to amuse me is the sight of African huts with satellite dishes crudely attached to their conical thatched roofs! It seems no matter how bad things are by way of food shortages and other necessities, TVs and mobile phones are a must, even out in the bush! Curious as to how they get their power, I was told the huts belong to farm laborours who take their power from the main grid.

Nearing the Zambezi Valley I noticed what I thought were flags dotted around the bush and was told these blue and black screens are used in the Tsetse fly count. Also known as the Tik-Tik fly, a bite from one of these infected with the Trypanosoma Brucei Rhodesiense parasite causes Sleeping Sickness, the symptoms - weight loss, fatigue, fever, seizures, difficulty with balancing and walking, to name a few - usually appearing a couple of weeks or so after infection. The illness cannot only lead to a coma but can also be fatal. I recall in the 1950's cars being sprayed inside and out with DDT from a hand spray which I can only describe as a refillable tin can attached to the end of a pumping tube.

Turning off the main road at Makuti (meaning '*wet mist*') we weaved our way on winding roads down to Lake Kariba, arriving at Andorra Harbour at about mid-day. We were met by Don and Nat, Cyn's sister and brother-in-law, both Zimbabweans, who had travelled from Zambia where they now live, to join us on the houseboat. Our crew consisted of three local Zimbabweans – MacDonald the Captain, Philemon the cook and Tafadzwa the deckhand. Once the houseboat was loaded we set sail for Chinga where we docked for the night. Before supper we got on the small speedboat 'Kafupi' meaning 'Shorty' which towed behind the houseboat and had sundowners on the lake. As we bobbed on the water we watched Impala roaming the shoreline. These timid animals are prolific and happily co-exist with the baboons which, like the elephant, hippo and crocodile are also plentiful.

Elephants on shoreline, Chinga

The following day we left Chinga and sailed for Palm Bay, named as such due to a scattering of Palm trees along the shoreline. It was only after setting sail from Chinga we looked back and noticed a group of elephants coming out of the bush down to the water. Disappointed we had missed them we asked Don if he would take us back in Kafupi to get a closer look. It was heaven being so close to these majestic beasts and after much clicking of cameras we departed, catching up with the houseboat for G&T's and lunch.

Going along, the little swallows and wagtails living under the pontoon-style houseboat would zip in and out over the water catching various tiny insects one couldn't see with the naked eye. Approaching Palm Bay we saw elephants and hippos on the shoreline. Once moored, we again went out on the lake and had sundowners on Kafupi as we watched the sun go down.

The following day I joined the men on a fishing trip. After finding a suitable spot John tethered the boat to a tree, branches of petrified wood standing proud of the water, remnants from the valley being filled with water in the 1950s, creating what is now known as Lake Kariba, at that time the largest man-made lake in the world. There is a threat to the lake at present with its dam wall swelling risking cracks in its structure. The collapse of the wall would send about 180 billion cubic meters of water downstream posing a risk to roughly 3.5 million people in Zimbabwe, Zambia and Mozambique.

Once the boat was tethered, Neil dropped the anchor, a huge boulder on a rope. Other than Neil catching a fair sized bream we caught very little, however, just being on the lake close to the wildlife on the shore and hearing the cries of the fisheagles overhead made it all worthwhile.

Fisheagle

When the heat became unbearable we packed it in and headed back to the houseboat for a hearty brunch before cooling down in the pool – a crocodile-proof cage lowered off the back of the boat into the lake. It was here we took the opportunity of shampooing our hair as well!

Another fishing trip later that afternoon saw Neil catch an impressive bream. I managed to catch a fish called a Squeaker, named as such due to the sound they make. I had never seen such an ugly fish in all my life so was quite pleased when, after trying to land it, it slipped the hook, diving back into the water! When we decided to head back to the houseboat Kafupi wouldn't start no matter how hard Don tried. We realized the only thing for it was to row back. However supposedly only having one oar - the other being discovered a day later! - the men had to take it in turns rowing on one side and then the other zig-zagging our way back to the houseboat. I couldn't do much so volunteered sitting up front as the SatNav! It didn't help when Cyn's rendition of "row, row, row your boat" carried across the water!

Setting sail the next day we headed for another spot on Palm Bay, negotiating the branches of petrified wood, some of which housed cormorant nests. As we approached the bank and before tethering the houseboat to the trees on the island, a crocodile slid through the bushes down the sandy bank before raising itself on its legs and walking swiftly down to the water, slipping away into its depths. I thought the crew very brave going on land to tie the ropes to the trees, thus securing the houseboat. As we relaxed in the searing heat of the afternoon, some reading books, some napping, we could hear the grunts of the hippos and the intermittent deep moan of a lion, almost as if it were chiding or admonishing its young. Later in the evening whilst having supper we heard lions again, this time roaring, their sound carrying over the water from the Matusadona National Park on the mainland. That night we fell asleep to the distant sound of the 'Lion's Lullaby'. In the early hours of the morning the wind picked up and we awoke to the boat rocking to and fro. Tafadzwa said the boat was 'dancing' which we all thought pretty apt!

The next day before setting sail for Antelope Island for our final night before returning to Andorra Harbour, Nat and I went onland – yes, the very spot we saw the crocodile! – to collect smooth stones and pebbles for her water feature back home. We also took a quick boat ride in Kafupi and came across a huge pod of hippo, their heads popping out of the water as they eyed us suspiciously. Hippos are the biggest killer in Africa and the last thing we needed was to upset them. Cyn began to panic and begged Don to move on saying *"this is the last place we want to be if Kafupi packs in!"*, how right she was!

Hippos

That night on Antelope Island the wind picked up bringing with it a brief but torrential tropical storm with thunder and lightning. At daybreak the boat was more than 'dancing', this time it was 'rocking 'n rolling'!

White horses began to appear on the choppy waters which meant a delay in our departure from Antelope. Nat said she'd never seen anything like it to which Tafadzwa replied *"For me too, what a surprise!"*!! Our attempt to cross the lake proved futile and after an hour or so we had to turn back to Antelope, taking shelter in a different bay. Taking in the beautiful scenery we suddenly spotted a family of baboons hopping along the rocky shoreline towards us. There were five of them, two youngsters, dad, mum and a newborn which clung tightly to mum's underbelly.

Mum and newborn

Knowing these opportunists well we all kept a keen eye on them as they sat eyeing the boat out. It was just us girls on the back of the boat when dad suddenly made his move. Had any men been around he wouldn't have been so brash but they're not afraid of females. We all screamed as he grabbed the back railing peering through it at the tasty salted fish drying out which the cook was taking home to his family. The cook came running out of the kitchen and shoo-ed him away. Returning to his spot on the bank dad continued to eye us out. Normally we wouldn't feed them as it would be unkind if they were to rely on humans for food, but this time we threw them orange skins taken from the now over-flowing dustbin on the back of the boat and a bit of sadza which the cook shared from his plate. That night provisions weren't plentiful but Cyn, being resourceful, managed to rustle up boerewors (spicy sausage) and sadza for supper.

At about 5.30 the next morning we were all still asleep when the engines roared into life and we set sail, hoping this time we would make it across. It was still dark and we could see the twinkling lights of Kariba in the distance. The crossing was pretty hairy with the houseboat rocking this way and that. Not far from the mainland I began to feel extremely nauseous and just about made it from the top deck downstairs to the toilet where I threw up. I lay down for the remaining part of the journey and as soon as we moored in the harbour I fled the boat, happy to be on terra firma again! We said our goodbyes waving off Don and Nat as they made their way back to Zambia and Neil, Cathy and Betty as they made their way to Tiger Safaris about 60 kms away where they would spend a couple of nights before returning to Harare.

Back in bustling Harare I began to think about my return to the UK. Souvenirs are always a must and Cyn kindly drove me to a local market in what we now call 'the Harare Ferrari', named as such after Betty said it sounded like a Ferrari when starting up. The trusty old Datsun 120Y, mentioned in my first book published in 2014, is still going strong and is still the centre of attention wherever we go. Not quite a classic, with another three years before being classified as such - the car that is, not Cyn! - locals clamour around begging to buy her. Most supermarkets have security in their car parks and invariably the Harare Ferrari always got special treatment. Posh Mercs and 4x4s didn't stand a chance against the dated clapped-out Datsun which was singled out by security guards, recompensed generously, who considered her worthy of protection.

At the market rows and rows of colourful stalls stood side by side, each stall holder desparately trying to draw us in as we walked by. I marvelled at the array of locally made goods and, after watching workers turn a bit of wire into something quite equisite, I wondered how these people were able to make something out of nothing. Taking in the colourful array of goods I noticed what looked like Christmas decorations, stars made of wire and beads and little wire angels, all displayed in long lines. The stallholder explained "*We don't have Christmas anymore, but one day it will come back"*, a poignant moment which touched me deeply. Picking up a red star I promised him I would hang it on my tree every Christmas so I can look at it and pray for Christmas to return to Zimbabwe.

Completely forgetting my Shona for 'too expensive' and instead of saying *'Aah chadura!'* I mentioned my retired status which had the stallholder calling me 'Gogo', meaning 'Granny', "*Gogo, look at this, special price just for you!*" as he eagerly led me this way and that. Market traders such as these don't do too badly and, certainly, this particular one did very well out of me! Their preferred method of payment is the much sought after US dollar, brought into the country mainly by tourists or the diaspora, Zimbabweans living and working outside the country. It is believed a quarter of Zimbabweans make up the diaspora. Without their own currency, Zimbabwe now use Bond Notes, not worth anything, which the locals call 'Mickey Mouse' money, however, even these are in very short supply resorting to most payments being made electronically (eco-cash) for which there is an extra charge. Save for the US dollar and the odd Bond Note in circulation it seems to me Zimbabwe has become a cashless society with a worthless eco-cash system just going round and round within its borders. How the locals manage is beyond me. Many walk the streets trying to sell what little produce they have while others set-up makeshift stalls on road corners in the suburbs. The current cholera outbreak which started on the outskirts of Harare where water wells and boreholes were contaminated with sewage, has resulted in a national emergency with hawkers/vendors of fruit and vegetables being driven out of the city. By the time I left Zimbabwe on 15 September some 3,000 people had been infected by the cholera and typhoid-causing bacteria with 25 people, mostly in Harare, dying.

I always leave Zimbabwe with a heavy heart but this time, as I wished the airport staff well in dealing with this new catastrophe, my heart felt like lead. How much more can these people endure? Their resilience and cheerfulness knows no bounds, even in adversity such as this.

After boarding the plane and taking my seat I have a little ritual I always play out in my mind. I close my eyes, relishing the last few moments I am still on Zimbabwe soil, albeit just the wheels of the plane and, after take-off, I look back on the lights of Harare, craning my neck until I can see them no more before being enveloped in the darkness of Africa.

Epilogue

Its early October 2018 and I'm back in the UK. How things change in just a few weeks. As I write, the Zimbabwe Finance Minister has announced plans for a 2% tax on money transfers. A short few weeks ago whilst in Zimbabwe the exchange rate was two Bond Notes to the US dollar, now I'm told its 125 Bond Notes to US$1,000! I was surprised at how well the supermarkets were stocked, however goods came at a price very few could afford. Hyperinflation is on the march and in order to protect their stocks in the hopes things will improve some supermarkets have closed their doors. The ones that still remain open have stopped pricing goods and its only when you get to the till you find out the cost of your shop. You know how dire things are when one citizen queuing for fuel said *"Perhaps Mugabe wasn't so bad after all"*!. Although I experienced the odd power cut whilst there I'm told power is now on and off throughout the day. A shortage of medicines, compounded by the current cholera epidemic, heightens the massive problems Zimbabweans are facing.

President Mnangagwa's promise of a new era of growth and stability has, unsurprisingly, fallen flat. Locals worry that their savings will be wiped out again, something that has happened three or four times already. The sad thing is there are so many capable

Zimbabweans waiting in the wings to reverse what has become a total catastrophe but, as we saw in July, vote-rigging and intimidation still play a major part in so-called 'free and fair' elections.

Only the people of Zimbabwe can change things but they can only do so if they're given a fair crack of the whip and greater transparency.

ISBN 978-1-912505-41-8

BV - #0017 - 171218 - C13 - 210/148/7 - PB - 9781912505418